A Pocket Guide to
Habit Change

Liz Myers

A Pocket Guide to Habit Change

Written by Liz Myers

Edited by: Kathlyn H. Stewart

Cover design: Kay Williams

The author of this book does not dispense medical advise or prescribe the use of any technique as a form of treatment for physical, emotional, or medical problems without the advice of a physician, either directly or indirectly. The intent of the author is only to offer information of a general nature to help you in your journey for emotional, physical, and spiritual well-being. In the event you use any of the information in this book for yourself, the author assume no responsibility for your actions.

Contents

Introduction

As I strolled along the street, I could detect the hint of a familiar smell wafting in the distance. A feeling arose immediately, which felt like an intense longing for something that wasn't there. It was the smell of tobacco swimming through the air and landing in my nostrils. It's amazing how powerful that simple smell was and how easily it could take me out of my lovely nature walk and place me right back into the not-so-distant craving for an old habitual practice.

Have you ever had that experience? You are minding your own business and suddenly a wave of aromatic pleasure/memory/habit hits you right in the nose?

I used to talk quite a bit about malls and how they pumped that yummy aroma of freshly baked cinnamon bread right through the walkways. And just like that, you'd be chewing on the fresh two-for-one bread special that just tasted way too good to keep up with the deal you made with yourself to eat only gluten-free and organic.

And there you were, going against your own promise to yourself again: torn between feeling great because it tasted so good and then later feeling bad because you let yourself down again. Maybe you spent time rationalizing the decision or, worse, beating yourself up for giving in. Either way, why spend so much energy and time on something that lasted less than five minutes to enjoy? The main reason: habits. The other reason: agreements. We will dive into this habit game and break it all down into good chunks of helpful information for you to digest, practice and enjoy. And the good news is, **you are in complete control of your choices if you choose to be!**

I know because I practice this shit. As a fellow human who's gone through her own battles with overhauling unhealthy habits and addictions, I understand this process can be quite challenging, yet, I also know it is more than worth it! I am not a preacher; just a simple teacher, and I promise to be real with you about this process of habit change.

Just so you know where I am coming from, let me share a bit about my background knowledge, training and experience as it relates to habit change. Formally, I have my Master of Arts degree in Counseling with an emphasis on substance abuse and mental health counseling. I hold several mindfulness-based life coaching and wellness-coaching certifications. I've been coaching, counseling and teaching others in this field for about 20 years now! I am a trauma-informed yoga and meditation teacher as well. In addition to all this formal training, I've struggled over the years with my own battle with alcohol addiction, co-dependency, food addiction, persistent negative thinking and cigarette smoking. All great stuff for a book on habit change, don't ya think?!

Through all of my ups and downs with releasing myself from addiction, self-criticism and judgment, I've found the "middle way" to be the key to my success. I've applied the concepts of self-love and moderation as the guiding forces to my recovery. I can say that I no longer have a drinking problem, and cigarettes have taken their final boot to the curb. I have learned to recognize when co-dependency is creeping in again. As far as food goes, it's soooo wonderful, isn't it?! I've gone through restricting food because I thought I was "fat." I then lost weight and went too far the other way and was "thin," but unhealthy. Then I went back the other way--using food to cope with life and my emotions again--and gained all the weight and then some back. So, I got lots of therapy and learned how to find the weight and body type that works for me and my lifestyle. I found the moderation way and I am quite happy about how I look and feel from the inside out. I also listed "persistent negative thinking" as a habit I've changed because it's essential to remember that thought processes and "thought trains," as I like to call them, are a huge part of this change process game! I may still have negativity from time to time, but it's not something that is attached to so many aspects of my life anymore. I've been able to see how perception is so much of the initial battle to make changes and seeing the glass half full was something I decided I had to figure out if I wanted to enjoy my life.

I think that's enough about me for now. Throughout this book, I will share more examples so you know that I am right there with you.

I know that you absolutely CAN change whatever it is that you would like, but you MUST learn to accept yourself and your situation just the way it is now or none of this will work!

So, before we move forward, please say this out loud with me. "I love and accept myself just the way I am now."

Okay, now say it again, and try to mean it this time, **"I love and accept myself just the way I am now."** And then remember to not add the "but" at the end of the sentence; instead, just say it and place a period there.

"I love and accept myself just the way I am now, period."

One more thing: please do yourself a favor and grab a pen and a journal. I will have questions for you throughout this book that will help you to understand your habitual patterns, break them, and create new ones that will support you well. To make it easier on you, I've put the most important questions at the end of each short chapter, so when you finish the chapter, you can get to writing yourself. How cool is that?!

As you move through this book, take it slowly and see which strategies are right for you and which ones are not. And remember, change takes time and effort, so one thing at a time is best!

Chapter 1

Interrupt and Disrupt Habitual Patterns

How old are you now? I know many people prefer not to be asked this question so I will rephrase. How old is your habit? How old is your pattern? Really think long and hard about the answer to these questions. It had to start somewhere and it usually started much further back than you think.

It can help to do what most of us humans do when trying to think about where something started: think about who you would like to blame for this habit? Who first introduced you to smoking? Drinking, and so on. Identifying who is to blame is a great way to start. Of course you will need to eventually blame yourself, but we will get to that later! Okay, so "blame" is a bit harsh. Let's say instead, who is responsible for teaching you this habit? It's also helpful to remember what was happening at the time you started this habit. How was life treating you at the time? Knowing where something originated and how long it's been around can be very helpful in understanding just how powerful and big this pattern has become. Something that has been around and has been reinforced on a consistent basis over many years will take some concentrated effort to alter and/or remove.

In order to make a breakthrough with this habit, we will need to use some trickery to get this situation moving and grooving. The key is to break up your current routine so you can create a new one that serves you better. We call this trickery "interrupting and disrupting your current patterns." It's like in the show, *Seinfeld* when the character Constanza decides to have an "opposite day" where he does everything opposite of what his instincts tell him to do. Interrupting and disrupting patterns is like having many "opposite days" in a row until your new way of being becomes your new way of living. You've got to turn the crank in the other direction and see what churns up. This may sound a bit wacky and uncomfortable and you are right because it is, at least in the beginning. But let me tell you that it is **so** powerful and it is worth it!

Take a moment now to look at your current routines and patterns and see where you need to make a disruption and/or interruption and do it. Then choose the number of days you will do this for. Many will refer to this type of strategy as a "cleanse" or a "detox"; taking space away from the item temporarily that has gone awry. Often this translates into a 7 day practice of abstinence. However, I also recommend 3- or 5-day breaks for those habits that have been around much longer and might need a shorter process this first time around. I highly suggest you find a handy dandy pen and journal and record your process. You may feel out-of-the-ordinary and a bit upside down for a while until you find your new way of operating. Remember, you got this! You can do it! Now it's your turn to get that pen moving.

Ask yourself:

- How old is my habit?
- Who introduced me to this habit?
- What was happening in my life when I started this habit? How was life treating me?

- ❀ When will I start my week of "opposite days" and/or detox time?

- ❀ How will I reward myself for my successful completion of this habit break/change?

Chapter 2

Discovering the Function behind the Habit

The habit or habits that are currently staring you in the face have some sort of function behind them. Ask yourself: Does the practice of this habit make me feel a certain way? Does it meet certain needs? Really think about it. We are often seeking a type of feeling or energy from the habit we are repeating. Are you looking for more energy? Are you looking to relax? Trying to get "high"? **Only when you decipher what function a habit is serving for you can you begin to let go of it!**

I remember the day I first picked up smoking. I was 21 years old and I was working as a Child Protective Service Worker for the state of New Hampshire. I would read reports all day long about suspected child abuse and/or neglect happening to these kids at the hand of their caregivers. Sure, I was there to protect and help; however, what I didn't realize was how overwhelming this type of work was, especially for someone as sensitive and intuitive as myself. About six months into the job, I already felt burnt out. I doubted my abilities to truly understand what was happening in these households and how to work with a system that felt more broken then the homes themselves. I mean, what did I really know at 21 years of age? I started to move into a depressed place and what did I find that might lift me out of this misery and doubt? Well, cigarettes of course! But American Spirits brand, because, you know, it's not like they are as cancerous as "regular" cigarettes! My co-worker had offered me one and I said, "Fuck it, life sucks anyway, I might as well enjoy smoking." There it started and, just like that, I dove in.

For the next six months, I smoked and I deepened my drinking habit. I was looking for relief. I was looking for connection to my co-workers. I was looking for a way to cope, and, in a weird way, I felt like I deserved to shorten my life since I was so miserable at the time. I felt like I was fighting a failing system and my heart was getting torn up. I quit that job once my one-year contract was up, but I carried the smoking habit with me. It went on for about four more years until I was forced to choose between having a successful surgery or smoking. You see, I had giant knockers. Yes, knockers refers to breasts! They were huge, about a size F, you know for "fucking" big. The surgeon said I could not smoke if I wanted things to heal right. So, I decided it was worth it to quit smoking.

That's part of my story. What's yours? Take note that most of us embark upon making a change once the doctor and/or the body demands it happen. And even then, we don't always listen. Maybe we are just not ready, or we're too fragile, scared and so on. What is squeezing you to make this change now? Is it your body begging for a change? Is it your spouse? Mother? Best friend? Conscience? Intuition? Maybe it's all of the above? Listen and believe in yourself. You are worth it.

Now take a moment to answer these questions:

Ask Yourself:

- ❀ What was happening in my life when I first decided to partake in this habit?
- ❀ Does this situation still exist in my life and does this habit help with it?
- ❀ Is there a certain feeling state or need I am trying to achieve with this habit?
- ❀ How else could I get this need/feeling state met?

Don't stress if you don't have clarity with the answers to these questions yet--it will come in time! Try to really be aware and focus on your habit over the next few days or weeks and notice what you discover. The answers will arise if you allow them and give your attention to objectively observing the functions of your habit. This is a compassionate process, so go easy on yourself with what you discover. The truth can set you free if you let it.

Chapter 3

Believe in Yourself and Your Self-Worth

Here we are with those touchy-feely concepts of self-worth, self-esteem, belief in yourself and so on. Yes, I am asking you to believe in yourself. Trust yourself. Find out why you are worth it. Has anyone outside of you ever made you doubt your worth as a human being? If you are more than a year old, I am sure you have experienced someone cutting you down and making you feel like "less than." We've all been there and believe me, it's not pretty. Sometimes it's not somebody else that is cutting you down, it's just ourselves being a big old bully. All I gotta say here is, you are worth it and you MUST believe this if you're going to change habits.

This is where emotions and bad days can cause some tricky scenarios along this habit change path. It's important to take some time to unveil the people, places, things and emotional states that may take you off your game or derail all your hard work and progress—also known as your saboteurs. Have you ever experienced a time when you set a new goal and you were doing great and then you had a fight with your significant other and you found yourself seeping into a "just fuck it" attitude? This is anger taking over. This is the saboteur in full effect. You've got to arm wrestle with this saboteur and tell it that this goal **does** matter and **you** matter and your goals **are** worth pursuing.

Here, we also need to pause to remember that bad moments in life happen and they can take you off your game. So, if your saboteur does win occasionally, no worries. The other key practice in this habit-change game is to go whole-heartedly into a space of forgiveness so the saboteur will only have a short stay instead of a continued stream of taking you down. Does that make sense? If it doesn't yet, no worries, we will circle back to forgiveness again. Here are some questions to keep the benefits of changing your habit in the forefront of your mind so that your saboteur will have less of a chance of derailing you.

Ask Yourself:

- How will eliminating this habit and/or reducing the frequency/amount of this habit benefit me?

- How will starting a new habit/lifestyle change benefit me? How might it benefit others?

- How do I know when my saboteur is present? What does it feel like?

- What makes my well-being worth it? What are all the reasons why I am more important than this habit (Please list 10 reasons)

Chapter 4

Adaptability and Flexibility

Ugh, adaptability AND flexibility, really Liz? Can't I just stick with my regular routines that are so familiar and cozy?! I hate to break it to you, but I know you are ready for a change or you wouldn't be reading this book right now. I know it can be tough to walk in a new direction, leave something behind or try something new. But remember, it can also be liberating, freeing and exciting to release the old so you can get that new mojo moving!

It's like getting rid of that old dusty memory-filled stereo that is asking to be let go of so you can enjoy songs on something that will play them without skipping a beat. You really don't know what you are missing until you take a step towards something new. However, there are no guarantees with your new direction and that is what often keeps us stuck in the complacency game. Did you know that the majority of people would not change doctors even if they have repeatedly received poor healthcare? It's astonishing how powerful the fear of the unknown can be! Human beings would simply rather stay in their comfort zone even if or when it has developed mold and mildew. Why? Because it's familiar. The mold in that comfort zone may be killing you, but hey, you know what it looks like and maybe you've grown fond of it. Maybe you simply don't even notice it any more. Get the picture?

I am sure you do and I know you are ready to break out of that moldy comfort zone and leap into something unknown. The first steps in your new direction can be liberating! But these initial changes can be tough to stick with because your old habit will be crying for your attention like you wouldn't believe. Just think of a poor chocolate cake with no one to eat it. It's just staring at you from the kitchen feeling all abandoned and sad. Don't let that cake's tears get you all bent out of shape. Let the cake cry itself to sleep. That's a ridiculous thought, I mean you know that someone else will just step up to the plate and eat the cake, smoke the cigarette, take the drink, and so on. There is always someone else there that will partake in the habit, so don't worry your little head about the feelings of your habit.

So, let's get real and get to a helpful tip here. It's called the three-time rule. Have you ever noticed that wishes come in three's? Have you ever heard that the "third time is the charm"? I am sure you have heard of the magic of the number three. Well, there really is something to this and it is one of the keys to your success. When you are trying something new, you've got to give it three chances. Now, you must take this advisement with discretion, as there are some things you will just know right away are not right for you. Let's take crack for instance; hopefully you will never try that, but if you do, please do not give it three chances to get ahold of you!

In all seriousness, let's think about walking away from the habit of smoking, for example. You will most likely need some type of "replacement" therapy for this habit in order to be successful. You could give chewing gum a try. Each time you have a craving for the cigarette, instead, you chew gum. The first time you go to try this technique, you may hear yourself saying something like this, "Really, gum? I am replacing the smooth drag of tobacco with this sugary chewy pathetic stuff? Come on, this just doesn't cut it."

Now, give that gum a chance. In fact you must give it at least three chances before you put it on the chopping block. It takes time for you to adjust and accept the new way of being. There will often be a natural comparison game and an itching for the new technique to be an underperformer. Give it time and know that it's natural for your inner child to be throwing a bit of a fit here. After you have given it a third try, ask yourself, is this working? If the answer even remotely resembles a "yes," then keep it up and add some variety, maybe a different flavor, ohhhh weee. However, if it feels more like a "no," then you can ditch the gum and try something else. It's important to mention that not all habits can be broken without some sort of physiological withdrawal. If your habit has reached the stage of true addiction or physiological dependency on the substance, then you may need to take this transition process even slower. I will give my example of how I slowly weened myself off of tobacco in chapter 8.

You may need to find additional supports to get you through this transitional process. You may need to join a group, get a sponsor, find a gym. Go back to what we started to explore in Chapter 2: What is the intent behind the habit? Is there something—a feeling or a need--it is covering up?

Okay, so this may sound a bit tedious but this process takes some work. This is where you may find the next phrase to be very helpful with your success.

"What you resist persists."

The more you resist something in your awareness, the more it seems to persistently knock you on your noggin', just begging to be heard. The habit you would like to change/break or incorporate is not something you can easily bury once you have that deepened awareness of it. Like a child poking you in the arm over and over again, it will annoy you and weigh on you until you take action. It's like you carry that energy inside that keeps speaking to you and sometimes even yelling at you to listen up and take action. And if that doesn't get your attention, your doctor, spouse or other loved ones will continue to get on your case until you take steps forward.

It will persist and the resistance could be used to push you forward instead of dragging you down.

Your turn!

Ask Yourself:

- ❀ Is there something I could temporarily replace this habit with?

- ❀ How will I utilize the three-time rule to help me with the transition away from my old habit into a new behavior?

- ❀ List two examples from your past where making a change in your life was worth the risk. What did I leave behind? What did I gain? How has this change benefited me in my life?

Chapter 5

Setting the Successful Stage

Let's get to the positive stuff, shall we?! In order to be successful, it's extremely helpful to know who will be your cheerleader and support you during this change process and who will not. Some folks like to encourage others on their path to change and others simply do not. Sorry to say it, but a lot of people like to swim in the negativity pool coupled with a stagnation nation floaty. As you find someone to share this change with, be very discerning about who that is. And know that you can always find new cheerleaders if you need them. You've got to protect your process from those who may not want nor be able to support you through this. If you have trouble finding someone, hire a professional or pull out your journal and get to writing. Most importantly, you are your best cheerleader! So you will need to try on some of these handy dandy helpful phrases.

- ❀ I got this.
- ❀ I can do this.
- ❀ I am strong.
- ❀ I am intelligent
- ❀ I will not give up.
- ❀ I am worth it
- ❀ It's worth it

Instead of an "Ask Yourself" section here, I invite you instead to "tell yourself".

Write five more helpful encouraging "cheerleader" type of phrases. Then put your list where you can easily see your phrases and access them as you need them. Accountability really does work, whether you utilize a coach, friend, counselor, journal, social media or some other mode; you've got to have that encouragement factor in there.

1. _____

2. _____

3. _____

4. _____

5. _____

Chapter 6

Options for Change

There are so many strategies you can use to create habit change in your life. I will highlight some of the most common and useful strategies I've tested to be tried and true with myself and with my clients. What is important with all of these strategies is to follow this ideology: Keep fear at a level where it cannot overtake you or your progress. Remember when I referred to fear earlier in this book? If you don't, no worries, but now you have to experience a science lesson. Do you know about the body and the ANS? No, not the A-N-U-S, the A-N-S, the Autonomic Nervous System. This basically refers to the automatic inner workings of the body and it is broken up into the PNS and SNS, otherwise known as the Parasympathetic Nervous System and the Sympathetic Nervous System. Since I am not a nurse nor a doctor nor a scientist, I will focus on the fear factor and basically how it operates in this system. In essence, the Parasympathetic Nervous System focuses on the "rest and digest" functions of the body. It kicks on when it's time to go to sleep, take a nap or digest your yummy food. It doesn't have much awareness of fear or high energy. It's like your good ole couch potato friend that may be inviting you to take a puff off that chill indica weed. In today's modern society of constant movement and striving, this system does not get a chance to kick in as much as it used to. On the other hand, we have the Sympathetic Nervous System, the one responsible for our "fight, flight, freeze" responses. This system is more of an alert system that kicks on for many reasons but most of them involve going out into the world, facing tigers and cutting in line to get your cup of buzz buzz coffee. It lets you know when there is a threat to your survival somewhere in your environment; it protects you and keeps you alert. Both the PNS and the SNS are quite beneficial to our well-being and functions. Both systems can also be detrimental to us if they don't each get a fair chance to operate.

Ask yourself:

Do I like to be busy and go and go? Do I enjoy adrenaline rushes and moving from one thing to the next? Or, do I like to relax and do nothing? How is my digestion? It's super helpful to notice if you reside a bit more in the land of lethargy and relaxation (Parasympathetic) or if you reside more in the go-go-go atmosphere (Sympathetic). There is no right or wrong here, just observations to see if you need to put in a little more time into movement or into stillness.

We started this science lesson by talking about this important suggestion, "**Keep fear at a level where it cannot overtake you or your progress.**" So, what does that mean? It means, don't let your SNS override your progress by freezing you or inviting you to flee or by fighting what you need to do. When taking on a new venture, you've got to make small steps that you can achieve otherwise this fear factor can take over and dismantle your whole plan. Of course you don't want to make these steps so easy that there is no challenge. However, you do want to make it so your steps slip just far enough under the fear radar so you can keep your change train chugging along. In other words, don't bite off more than you can chew because then your chew chew train will stop chugging along and you will be right back where you started. Remember, success builds upon success and feelings of being a failure, well, lead to feeling those low vibrations of failure. We all know that feelings of failure do not tend to lend a hand to making successful changes. And don't you worry about how big or how small to make the steps. In this habit change process, there is much trial and error to be had, especially in the beginning. So you've got to give your action steps a try and learn from the process. If you discover the steps you made were too big, then revamp your plan and try again. If you find the steps were too small, then you've got some success already and you are well on your way to making them a bit bigger.

Ask Yourself:

- ❀ Do I enjoy adrenaline rushes and moving from one thing to the next? (also known as operating in the Sympathetic System)
- ❀ Do I like to relax and do nothing? (Parasympathetic System)

- Do I need to add in more time for my system to relax?

- Do I need to add in something to help my system to wake up?

- How can I keep fear at a level that it won't overtake my progress?

Chapter 7

Cold Turkey Method

O kay, now that we've got that fear factor figured out, here are some other suggestions and modes to explore. I am sure you have heard of the "cold turkey" method for quitting something. You just wake up and you say, "I am so fed up with you [fill in the blank with your habit here], never again will I do…never again will I be…" fill in these blanks. And just like that, you are done with the habit. You simply quit cold turkey! Now, a word of caution: though this method CAN work, it tends to be much more harsh and can really trigger your fear factor. It is something that tends to work for a temporary period of time until the old habit rears it head and demands its return in full force. Maybe you have tried to quit many times and have been temporarily successful in the past and this is the time that it will stick. I don't mean to be pessimistic about this method, but please only try it if you are sooooo done already with this habit and your mind and body are really ready to will it into place no matter what.

I often suggest instead that you use a modification of this cold-turkey method as an inspiration. Often, a shorter version or practice may be all you need to interrupt and disrupt the current habitual pattern. For example, say, "I will not drink coffee in the afternoon for the next three days." This is a modified form of the cold turkey method that allows you to see how strong the habit or addiction may be and it gives you a chance to keep the fear factor just under the radar. Simply put, it's more gentle and achievable.

Say you are interested in creating a new habit. Maybe you want to add more veggies to your lunch instead of having that side of chips. You could say, "Instead of having chips with my lunch for the next three days I will have a side salad instead." Then, on day Four, you decide what to do, keep going or have some chips and see how you feel.

Ask Yourself:

- Is there a habit I am sooo over and ready to quit completely?

- Is this habit something that I think I could stop doing for the next three days? If not, can I think of a modified version of lessening this habit, such as, "I will not smoke my first cigarette of the day before 10 a.m.?"

- How will I keep track of my progress and challenges with the strategy I choose to pursue with this habit change?

Chapter 8

Harm-Reduction Model

The harm-reduction method is something that is often used in rehabilitation treatments for drug users. Maybe that is what you are trying to get off of? Maybe not, but either way our habits can become addictions and when that is the case, you may need to first focus on reducing the harm to you versus quitting all together. You see, in my mind, the ultimate goal for habit change is longevity. That means that you may try several of these methods to change your habit and it may take many months or even years until you are able to really wrangle the beast, if you know what I mean! The important thing is that you keep trying, and the harm-reduction model could be a great way to begin making changes that will eventually become permanent.

Let's look at smoking as the example to view through this harm-reduction lens. I quit smoking in my 20's; remember that story from earlier when I discussed my big boobie reduction?! Well, I had a very challenging circumstance arise in my life in my late 30's and I started to "lightly smoke" those American Spirits again. Ya know, life can throw you some curve balls and my own decisions and actions created quite the curve ball of problems to deal with. So, what did I do, I went back to smoking. This time it lasted just two years, thankfully. Once I realized and acknowledged that going back to smoking was not in my highest good, I thought to myself, "How can I make it more challenging to smoke AND how can I reduce the harm to myself?".

The key component to the harm-reduction strategy refers to replacing part of the harmful activity with something that is not as harmful. In this instance, I decided it would benefit me to roll my own cigarettes and incorporate sage along with the tobacco. Sage is known for its mystical and relaxing effect. If I wanted to have a cigarette, I would need to take the time to roll one with less tobacco since nicotine is the most harmful and addictive component of the cigarette. Okay, so maybe that doesn't sound like a big step forward but looking at the long-term picture, it worked. I was able to see how much time it took to roll one of these sage/tobacco combos, thus showing me how much time this habit took up in my life. I was able to roll smaller cigarettes, which helped to reduce the amount of nicotine and smoke going into my body. I ended up smoking less because I didn't want to spend so much time making them. I did this for about one year and then, just like that, my smoking habit faded out completely. I was able to slowly wean myself off of the tobacco and incorporate more guidelines that made it difficult for me to get to the cigarette. And most importantly, it helped me to practice "delayed gratification." It's so easy just to grab a cigarette out of the box and smoke it. You think of it, you go get it and within seconds you are on your way to gratifying that need. With my example, I wanted it, but I had to put in some time and effort before I could receive the gratification of smoking. This delayed gratification is one of the essential keys to making lasting habit change. Each time I delayed smoking, I became stronger inside and my habit's power over me became weaker. I simply had to practice waiting.

This is one of the best strength-training tools you can have emotionally, physically and otherwise, and it's an incredibly powerful tool in overcoming habits!

Think about it: have you ever had a craving for something but you couldn't get to it right then? You then go about your day focusing on other things and by the end of the day you may have forgotten completely about that craving. Or, you may remember that craving, but you are too tired and/or unimpressed by it and you let it go. This makes you stronger against that craving. It shows you that you CAN let things go. Cravings are just a part of your mind that can pass if you let them. It's not always easy, but over time, you can take your power back.

Let's look at another example that relates more to emotional states instead of tangible items. Let's say you want to apply this harm-reduction concept to your anger management problem. Well, not you of course, this anger problem couldn't be from sweet you; it must be from someone else. Either way, let's take a look. So, you get angry at your significant other because of whatever annoying or disrespectful thing they did. You are angry and a blinding rage takes over and you say something quite unkind. Of course you didn't mean it, but you can't take firey anger you threw at your partner away now. Maybe you feel bad and you find a way to apologize but you know the damage has been done. You want to stop this cycle, so you say you will not get angry with your partner anymore but you really know better than that: You will get angry sometimes and it's really more about how you manage it. Let's manage it, shall we? With harm reduction, there are many ways you can go with this, but let's say when you feel anger arise, you will take yourself into another room and shut the door and yell in there until you can calm yourself down. That may not sound great, but it does break the habit of the anger arising and then throwing it up on your partner's face. Instead, it arises and you throw it up on your bedroom walls. There is still damage done, but the harm to self and others is much reduced. The idea here is to meet yourself where you are at and take steps to interrupt and disrupt your current pattern until you are ready to start better and healthier techniques. If you have had a long-standing habit of many, many years, it cant be broken overnight and expecting it to go that way is just another trap you will set for yourself and for others' expectations of you.

Ask Yourself:

- ❁ How can I delay my access to my habit by incorporating delayed gratification techniques?

- ❁ What step(s) can I take to reduce the harm of this habit?

- ❁ How might it benefit me to reduce the level of harm associated with this habit?

- ❁ How might it benefit others to reduce the level of harm associated with this habit?

Chapter 9

It Is Easier to Bring Something New in Than to Take Something Away

This can be referred to as "replacement therapy." Have you ever heard that most people don't ever break their habits or addictions, but simply switch to a new one? It's true, more science for you. You may have heard the dreaded fact about how most smokers will gain at least 10 lbs. when they quit. And why? Well, you know, cigarettes speed up your metabolism, but also, most people end up substituting that ciggy for food. If you want to quit something and not pick up something else that will bring you down, then choose carefully what you will temporarily or even long term replace it with. Most of us humans don't do well with empty space. It would be great if we could all just take something away and be okay with it. However, most of us need something else to put in its place so we don't try to fill that empty space by going back to the old habit or even to something worse. My favorite example of this involves food because food is great and I really like talking about it. Let's go back to the chip and veggie example I gave earlier. Say you want to quit eating chips at lunchtime. This concept will still allow you to have chips; however, you will have to add veggies too. It goes like this: when making your lunch plate, fill it up with the veggies first. You must put more of them on your plate then the chips. The idea is that you will fill up your plate with the new thing first so there is less room left for the old thing that you want or need less of.

Let's look at this from another angle. Say I want to clean up my language and use the word "fuck" just a bit less. I am sure you know what I am going to say next, right? What do you do, you replace that swear word with the word "fudge." Yeah, it's cheesy but it really works. You simply replace it and it's pretty easy to do.

Ask Yourself:

- ❀ What can I add more of that is better for me than the current habit I am trying to remove from my life?

- ❀ What can I temporarily replace this habit with?

Chapter 10

The Kaizen Way: One Small Step Can Change Your Life

H
ere we get to discuss one of my favorite book recommendations, *The Kaizen Way,* by Dr. Robert Maurer (April 22nd, 2014). This book helped me so much with so many changes and transitions because it really works. And it is a short read, which is one reason why I love it so much! We've discussed much of this already in regards to taking things one small step at a time but I really can't stress this enough. If you want long-term results, the slow process will make the change last. "The Kaizen Way" book refers to simply taking one less sip a day of that which you wish to eliminate. It may seem silly but this goes back to the concept about success building upon success and keeping fear at a level where it cannot override your process. For example, you can try

using one less swear word a day, one less angry outburst, one less cigarette, one less...you fill in the blank. This small step process strengthens your inner abilities and it allows you to really observe how much you are consuming and/or partaking in your habit.

Ask Yourself:

- ❁ How can I decrease the amount of this habit just a little bit today?

- ❁ What strategies can I implement to decrease the amount and/or frequency of this habit today?

- ❁ What would it look like if I had just a little bit less of this?

- ❁ If you are incorporating something new, ask yourself, how can I add this into my day just a little bit?

Chapter 11

Perfectionism Is Outdated

Yes, I am a perfectionist in recovery, how about you? I definitely have used perfectionism as a roadblock in many ways throughout my life. It has blocked my ability to try new things as I had this unrealistic expectation that I would have to do them perfectly the first time. It's blocked my ability to be vulnerable and real about my process with new learnings. It's put that all too powerful pressure upon a situation that really could have been enjoyable if I could have just let go of the stumblings involved in the process.

I invite you to go easy on yourself with this process of habit change so you don't create extra roadblocks that really don't need to be there. It can be helpful to go back to your childhood for this lesson. Remember yourself as a one-year-old child? Yeah, I don't remember either! Just try to go there and remember that you didn't always know how to walk. Yeah, you really didn't, isn't that incredible? If you are concerned about getting things right, remember that you did much of it wrong before you got it right. When your parent decided it was time for you to get walking, do you think you were able to just strut your one-year-old butt down the walkway? Ha, you wish! You stumbled and fell on your butt and you held onto furniture, relied on adults' hands for help and so on. Why would it be any different now? Just because you are in an adult body, it does not mean you "should know better" and/or know how to do this new thing already. Please allow yourself to be just like that little child learning how to walk for the first time. You will need supports (people and things), you will get it wrong, you will stumble, and you will have to get up time and time again until you get it right. And even when you do get it right, you will have days when it will go all wrong. But the idea is that it is worth keeping at it because walking is amazing! Similarly, that's why you've got to nail in your "why it's worth it" inventory. We touched upon this in Chapter 3 when we addressed the need to believe in yourself and your self-worth. It's easy to see why walking is worth it. But can you remind yourself why thinking more positively is worth it? Why quitting smoking is worth it? Why being more kind to others is really worth it? You get the picture. Get those one-year-old legs moving and remember that you are like that one-year old, not that perfectionistic adult that already knows better. Be prepared to know nothing and you will fare much better.

Ask Yourself:

- Do I have perfectionistic tendencies?
- How will I utilize the one-year-old-trying-to-walk analogy to soften my change process?
- What supports or tools might I need to help myself?
- What are all the reasons why I am worth it?
- What are all the reasons why it (the habit change) is worth it

Chapter 12

As You "Let Go to Let Grow," Sometimes You Feel Growing Pains

We were discussing using your one-year-old legs in the last chapter. Now we will address your inner child. Have you done the "inner child" exercise before? If not, here is your chance. If so, let's get this kiddo connection party started, shall we?! All you have to do is picture yourself as a child. Really connect with what you looked like, picturing your hair color, hair length, clothes, shoes, and your age. Do your best and pull it into your awareness what it felt like to be this kiddo. Now, you may ask, well what age am I supposed to be, Liz? The answer is: Whatever arises when you look at your little self, is the age you are supposed to

49

connect to. Mine is a blonde little six-year-old girl, which is quite interesting since my hair turned brown the year after.

As you begin to let go of your habit or "let go to let yourself grow," be aware that you will likely experience growing pains. These can show up in many ways. Often, they will take the form of resistance. You know your inner child is throwing a fit when he/she mutters "But I don't wanna" at you. It's your inner child who usually is the one that experiences the fear when you start to try and change a habit, and it's your inner child who causes the most resistance. So you've got to check in with them and support them through this somewhat scary change process. And how do you connect with this inner child? Well, you take the time to sit quietly and pull up the childhood image of yourself we just talked about, and have your "adult you" talk to your "little you." This inner child talk may sound a bit crazy but it really works. You may be wondering what you would say to this little you.

Think in terms of how you might comfort a little child if they fell off their bike. Would you scold the child for not getting it right? Would you encourage the child to brush it off and get back on the bike? Would you tell them it's time to quit because it's just too dangerous? Whatever the answers are for you, take note of what they are now and then see if you need to make any changes. Our inner child needs nourishment, kindness and guidance.

You will first ask yourself questions to get to know how you have been treating your inner child. Then you will ask yourself questions to support this inner child well. Please do not skip over these vital questions!

Ask Yourself:

- Did I answer the questions Liz just asked in the paragraph above?
- What observations do I have about how I treat my inner child?
- Are there any changes I would like to make about how I treat my inner child?
- Does my inner child need more support? Love? Encouragement? Boundaries? Discipline?

These questions may seem a bit intense; however, you've got to know if you are currently providing encouragement and support and/or if you are offering anger and blame. You may be providing all of the above. Whatever the answers, it's okay. This is simply a starting point to understand how you may be working with your inner child and how essential this is to your habit-change process.

Chapter 13

Practice Delayed Gratification

We touched on this earlier in this book, however, it is such a powerful tool to utilize in your journey of transformation that we must address it in more detail. In today's fast-paced society of quick fixes, band-aid approaches and fast cars, it's so easy to click a button and have something arrive at your doorstep with little waiting time. The idea behind delayed gratification is that you will receive that gratifying feeling, yet you will need to wait for it. Remember that little old thing called "patience"? Being willing to wait, being willing to let a craving pass, and understanding that you DO have power over your thoughts and your body are the keys to your mastery of your self and your habits!

Let's go to the example section, shall we?! I shared earlier in this book about my transition from smoking cigarettes to rolling smaller ones to then quitting smoking. Well, the strategy to roll the cigarettes built in a delayed-gratification factor because it delayed my ability to simply start smoking a cigarette when I wanted to. I had to put in time and effort before I could get that satisfactory moment. Let's look at another example. Say you have a strong craving for chocolate after breakfast but you are trying to break the habit of having sweets after every meal. All you've got to do is delay the craving, meaning you can make a general rule that after breakfast you will not have chocolate but you can have it sometime later in the day. Each time you wait until later in the day, you get stronger than the craving because you teach yourself (and the chocolate craving!) that you do not need to take action on the craving: you can simply let it stay as a thought. You can put time and space between you and the object of your desire and you can be okay. You might not be super happy about it at first, but the more you do it, the more you are able to see that when you divert your attention to other things, that craving thought can pass, so much so that you may not even remember later on that you had the craving in the first place!

Now, if you find this to be challenging, don't fret, I got you boo! It can be helpful to pair this delayed-gratification technique with the fact that putting something new in is easier than taking something away. For example, one of the things I suggest is to keep your hands busy doing other things, especially when it comes to quitting or lessening certain foods and other substances. Let's say that, after breakfast, you make a new routine of playing cards right after you eat so you can let your food digest and you can keep your hands busy and thoughts occupied. If the cravings are very strong, it can be helpful to remove yourself from gaining easy access to the object you are trying to eliminate and/or distance yourself from. So, you might start going for a walk outside right after breakfast.

These examples bring together the two concepts of starting something new/good for you and delayed gratification, which is quite the dynamic duo. Another way to really dive into understanding cravings and your thought patterns is through meditation. I haven't always been into meditation, however I do utilize it on a daily basis in my life presently. I cannot put into words how powerful it is to simply sit and observe the mind. And then to also notice how well you can observe your thoughts and then let them pass like clouds passing in the sky. The more you do this, the more you are able to notice what "thought trains" you may have running through your mind. And the more you can practice understanding that thoughts are just that, thoughts. Without action, a thought has no real power over you.

Ask yourself:

- ❀ What craving thought do I have that could benefit from utilizing this delayed gratification technique?

- ❀ What strategies will I use to practice delayed gratification with this craving?

- ❀ How can I combine the delayed-gratification technique with the adding-something-new-in technique to help me with habit change?

Chapter 14

Forgiveness If You Go Back to the Habit

P unishment, damnation, judgment. Do you like these words? Do you like how they feel? Neither do I, so why do we use this ammunition against ourselves so much? As you may know, these words are the opposite of the lovely concept of forgiveness. When you forgive yourself or someone else, it does not mean that you condone your or their behavior, it means that you are unwilling to carry toxic feelings towards yourself or another. We all know that toxic energy tends to lead to more use and abuse of substances and repetition of the behavior we are trying to change. The best thing we can do when it comes to moving forward is to forgive. I am not saying this is easy; sometimes it's really hard. Maybe you are not ready to forgive, maybe holding onto the toxicity is what you are used to. However, forgiveness and becoming less critical of yourself are ESSENTIAL to mastering your habits! Time and time again, I have witnessed folks make amazing transformations and time and time again I have witnessed these same people beat themselves up at nauseum if they have a misstep, if they take a wrong turn or slide backwards. The process is rarely linear, so you might as well look up some geometry and check out what fun shapes you may be drawing on the earth with your path! I also invite you here to try on this healing prayer from the Hawaiian culture called, "Ho'oponopono", which means, **"I am sorry, please forgive me, thank you, I love you."**

Say it as many times as you need to until you feel it and believe it so you can spend your energy on getting back on track towards achieving your goal. Please DO NOT utilize your change process as an opportunity to beat yourself up. Please DO utilize your transformation journey to practice forgiveness and believe in yourself and trust in your process.

Ask Yourself:

- ❀ Do I tend to beat myself up when I do not accomplish what I set out to do?

- ❀ How will I incorporate forgiveness into this change process?

- ❀ What words of support can I give myself if I go off track?

Chapter 15

Meditation

Meditation has quite a few varying definitions attached to it so I will do my best to share my understanding and use of it. Simply put, it's a practice of being with yourself in an observational and focused state. You can practice meditation by sitting in silence, listening to a guided meditation, engaging in mindful walking, as well as many other styles and options. If you are a very active person, you may want to start with a mindful walking meditation. This option is nice because you may have a very active mind and the walking can help to support your ability to slow down and focus. Mindful walking is done while walking slowly and it's often done in nature. While walking, do your best to first notice your breath, feel yourself breathing in and out, then notice the colors, scents, sounds around you and the earth beneath your feet. The idea is to focus on the present moment and to be with what "is" instead of thinking about all the "to do's" you have coming down the line.

When engaging in meditative practices, your mind will most likely bring your attention into the past or the future and that is fine. What you will need to do is cultivate enough awareness to catch yourself going into those spaces and then you can take a breath and remind yourself to come back to the present moment. This can be challenging at first; however, it is worth it! The more you practice, the more you can observe how easily your mind may move out of the present moment. This can also show you the general content of your thoughts and where your mind tends to wander. As you practice meditation, you can also go deeper into spiritual connection. As you center more into the present moment, you can ask to connect with your "higher self" or "inner guide." It gives you the opportunity to sit with yourself and go deeper to uncover where your intuition is guiding you.

The "Loving Kindness" meditation is one of my favorite meditations and it is linked to the need to practice forgiveness for successful long lasting changes to occur. There are quite a few variations of this meditation out there; however I especially love this one. If you are listening to the audio book version, then lucky you gets to receive a bit of my singing for this one! If you happen to want a different version then what I am offering here, simply look up the "Loving Kindness" meditation on YouTube or elsewhere on the internet and you will find many options. As you are ready, you will find a comfortable spot to sit or lie down and repeat these words and see what arises. I suggest you journal a bit about your experience afterwards.

The Loving Kindness Meditation:

Part I

Once you have found a quiet relaxing space, notice your next three breaths. Then, take three more breaths and make them just a little bit slower and longer. Then say (either out loud or inside to yourself) the following wishes:

> **"May I be well"**
>
> **"May I be happy"**
>
> **"May I be peaceful"**
>
> **"May I be loved"**

Repeat these four short phrases again two more times through. Simply notice how it feels to go through these loving wishes.

Part II

Bring into your awareness someone that you care deeply about and who cares about you. This can be a person or a pet, someone who is alive or whom has passed on. Take time to truly bring the image of this person or pet into your heart. Then say (either out loud or inside to yourself) the following wish for this being:

"May you be well"

"May you be happy"

"May you be peaceful"

"May you be loved"

Repeat these four short phrases again two more times through. Simply notice how it feels to send these loving wishes out.

Part III:

Finally, bring into your awareness someone who you have a small conflict with at this time or a situation that could use some loving kindness, perhaps forgiveness. Just like you did before, take the time to bring this person into your heart space. This may be challenging, but simply observe what arises. With this person in your awareness, say out loud or inside to yourself:

"May you be well"

"May you be happy"

"May you be peaceful"

"May you be loved"

Repeat these four short phrases again two more times through. Simply notice how it feels to send these loving wishes out to someone with whom you have a small conflict.

Part IV

Wrap this up by repeating these wishes to yourself one more time:

"May I be well"

"May I be happy"

"May I be peaceful"

"May I be loved"

Notice how you feel and if anything has shifted for you. Take a moment to write a few observations down. If it was helpful, then please utilize this often. If it was not helpful, well then don't do it again. Be honest with yourself. Wishing you loving kindness from my heart to yours!

Ask Yourself:

- ❀ Take some time to journal about your experience and ask yourself the questions below if you would like to take it one step further.

- ❀ How might meditation serve me? If you are already meditating, what are its benefits?

- ❀ Is there an activity I like to do that acts as a meditative practice for me?

- ❀ If you don't meditate, will you pursue some resources to give it a try? If so, when will you research those resources?

Chapter 16

Grief and Loss

Ugh, yes we must address grief and loss. There are two parts to the process of looking at these issues.

First, please take a moment and notice if the initial habit you are trying to break may have started from a loss: loss of a loved one, a job, a home, a pet, and so on. We touched on this earlier, so you may already have a clear understanding if this habit started around the same time that you experienced loss in your life. If not, keep listening, because grief and loss can really alter our paths, sometimes for good and other times for the not-so-good. If you notice that your old habit began during a time of grief or loss then you may notice that as you let go of this habit, the underlying feelings that were being covered up by the habit will start to rise up to the surface. Please see this as an amazingly positive, helpful and growthful experience.

I hear you saying, "But Liz, I don't want to go back and relive that pain. I don't want to experience that situation, those emotions again." Just know that some tribulations stick with us and much of it is covered up by habits, being busy and so on. Taking the time to uproot something that has been sneakily lying just under the surface will give you the opportunity to dive into true healing. It may not feel good at first, but the end result will be a freeing that is indescribable. In order to let go of something long-term, you cannot just heal it on the surface; you've got to allow yourself to go deep and truly release it. This is when I recommend that you get personalized coaching or counseling to support you through this process, that is, if you realize the habit you are trying to break or lessen came from coping with something much deeper. Let's take a deep breath here and take a moment to write down any action steps you may need to take.

Ask Yourself:

- ❀ Do I need to contact a friend and ask for a counselor or coaching referral?
- ❀ Do I need to call my health insurance carrier and get a recommendation for a practitioner?

Remember that calling to ask for a referral does not mean you will start counseling the next week. Just explore it and know that it takes time to set these things up. And please don't delay and get as much support as you can. Why? Because you deserve it.

Part II of this grief and loss discussion has to do with a different kind of grief and loss, that which arises from leaving the old habit, the old you, the old way, the old taste behind. You and others may experience this loss and feelings of grief. Think of your drinking buddies. What if you decided to quit drinking for awhile or another wonderful idea, decrease the amount that you drink? How much would your drinking buddies like that and/or accept that? If they are somewhat less than supportive, you may also need to experience a temporary or even long-term loss of spending time with these buddies. Many of the habits we perform are not just for us; they are also linked to others. Not everyone will support what you are doing and some of those folks will pressure you in the opposite direction than you want to go. You may find that your attachment to your old identity may pressure you into doing the opposite of your new direction. You see, most of us do not like to experience grief, loss and emptiness. The old you—the one linked to your habit-- will want to fight for itself. It does not really want to take on this new way of being, even if the new you wants it to. You may experience some real in-between craziness for a period of time as you grieve the old you while you awkwardly step into the new shiny you.

Ask Yourself:

- Was there a loss I experienced that led to the creation of this habit?
- What supports do I need to assist me while I go through some of these underlying feelings of grief and loss?
- Who supports me in this new venture?
- Who and what and where might I need to take space from temporarily while I make this change?

Chapter 17

Have Your Reasons of Worth in View at All Times

E arlier in this book, we identified some of your key reasons as to why you are worth this change in your life. It's so great to uncover, discover and write down the reasons why this new path is worth walking upon. Putting it on paper adds another dimension to its existence in your life. Voicing it out loud adds yet another layer of power to this new movement forward. And then, of course, you must take action on a consistent basis to bring it all together. If you find that you have yet to write down and/or voice these reasons why you are worth it/why it's worth it, then please go back and redo Chapter Three. Then pause and start writing! It is imperative that you identify these worthiness factors so when those moments arise where you are having a bad day and you do not want to follow through with the changes you are making, you can revert to the helper list as to why you should not say "F" it. You know, those days where you just are feeling off of your game, where every driver on the road is being an a-hole and you just don't feel like doing what you said you were going to do. This list of worthiness is like your written "cheerleader "friend who is always there for you, especially on those types of days. And be sure to make the list visible so you don't have to go searching through your many journals to find it.

Ask Yourself:

- What will help me to override that just "F" it attitude?
- What are the reasons why I am worth it?
- What are the reasons why changing my habit is worth it?

Chapter 18

Set Your Boundaries and Practice Them

A hh, boundaries. Who or what do you need to set boundaries with? Some boundaries are complex and others are quite simple, yet the power behind them can be immense. As I write this, I am sticking to a simple yet powerful boundary that I set. You see, I am writing from home. How lovely is that? Also, how friggin' distracting can that be? Shall I focus on my writing goal or shall I do more laundry or wash more dishes? Gee, how the chores at home seem so delightful when I am faced with sitting down to accomplish my goal! Isn't' it funny how the grass seems greener on the other side when you are in the midst of changing your habits and your lifestyle?

Setting boundaries with yourself involves having an honest conversation with yourself about how avoidance factor(s) show up in your life. Are their certain goals you have pushed off over and over again? You know, where you say, "There's just no time for that now." I will have to say that, yes, there is some truth to the timing of things, yet if we really look at life, we know at the deepest level that all we have is the present moment. Wasting that gift of presence in order to pursue a time "maybe" for later is really just a bullshit way to live. So that may sound a bit harsh, but you know what I am saying, right? When will you start that gardening project? When will you create art? You must ask yourself WHY you are avoiding diving in? Are you afraid of something? Not sure if you will do it right? Not sure that others will approve? I know this is a lot of questions, but you really need to look into how avoidance factors may be preventing you from moving forward with that which you are drawn to.

As a "people pleaser" in recovery, I certainly know what it is like to push off my own "to do" list in order to please or serve others and their needs. What I have realized is that it IS possible to set boundaries and to honor my own needs and wants.

You must come to this realization, too, if you are going to be successful in changing your habits. What is remarkable is that setting boundaries also makes it possible to then show up for others in an amazing way because you are more filled up with enthusiasm and high-quality energy as a result of honoring your own soul's needs. How inspiring and magical is that?

What if we all set boundaries to honor our own radical self-care and our soul's true desires? And then sent that bright happy light of inspiration and dedication out to others? I believe the world would be a much happier and brighter place, for sure! Ask yourself, what have you been avoiding or putting off for "just the right time"? See what boundary or boundaries you need to set with yourself in order to take one small step towards making "Right Now" the right time. Then ask yourself how you will stay in integrity with yourself for the boundary you set. As you may know, not everyone likes change and others may push back on your boundaries. If you can remember that your light inside will become much brighter because you set that boundary, it will be much easier to stick with it. And those that don't get how vital it is to feed your own light so you can then go and feed the rest of the world, can go take a hike, mmmk?! Oh, and remember that "perfectionism is overrated" chapter? This definitely applies here. It may take some time to really understand what boundaries you need and how to integrate them over time. Knowing what distracts you is a process and you may notice that it's feeling states that can take you down. So, again, find a counselor or coach to support you through this process to let out more of the awesomeness that is you!

If you have any trouble with this section, take a look at how you spend your time. Do you really need to check your email 20 times a day? Do you really need to post on social media every day of your life? It's not just the 10 seconds it takes to create the post; it's also the mental space it takes up in your mind and your being. If time is a big avoidance factor for you, then take the time to track how you truly spend your time each day with one full-day tracker activity. Track what you do throughout the day. Write everything down, yes, everything! It sounds a bit crazy but, please do it if time is a barrier for you. This way you can truly understand how you operate and where you end up putting your energy throughout the course of each day.

And this goes back to boundaries: notice if you drop what you are doing in the moment because someone else asks something of you. You can have people wait a moment, you can take the time to center yourself and complete what you are doing. If you are a parent, this can be challenging. At times you really will have to drop what you are doing to care for a little one. However, that delayed-gratification technique we learned is a great tool for kids and adults alike! Kids that receive things time and time again without delay will often become inpatient and spoiled adults. That is the training. It's a balance though, right?! You don't want to be neglectful of your child but you don't want to sprint to their need every second of every day, for it can take away from their own developmental process.

Last, how often do you say what you mean and mean what you say? Notice how often you actually do what you say you are going to do. If you are good at this, keep it up: you are in integrity with yourself and your word, and your energy will keep you going well. However, if you notice you say a lot of awesome stuff but you rarely follow through with the action part, then you will need to pay careful attention here. There is a certain level of trust you must have with yourself and this is correlated to how often you keep the promises and agreements you make with yourself. If you are in the habit of breaking those agreements, boundaries, and promises with yourself, then you must start with the following journaling activity. Yes, I am asking you to journal! It is so worth the time to do this and it can take literally five minutes of your day. You will write about whatever you want, however it can be very helpful to include the things you said you were/are going to do. After you have done this daily five- minute journal activity for a couple of weeks, then go back and look at what you wrote. Go easy on yourself and take note of the thoughts that are taking over your headspace. Then you can see how those thoughts may be contributing to your ability to keep your agreements with yourself or not.

Does this make sense? When you say you are going to do something and then you don't, it's like you are letting down your inner child inside over and over again and your inner child then slowly learns that you are not to be trusted, that your words are full of fluff. This can lead to low self-esteem and/or continually feeling let down. The easy fix: don't say so much! Stop saying you are going to do something until you are ready to take one small step towards making it happen. You've got to focus on repairing the trust with yourself, your words, and your actions.

This chapter has been packed full of opportunities for self-inspection, so get ready for a bunch of questions to support you in this amazing process of change!

Ask Yourself:

- ❀ What boundaries do I need to set with myself in order to make progress towards my goals?
- ❀ What boundaries do I need to set with others?
- ❀ What is the current level of integrity between my words and actions? Do I say what I mean and mean what I say?
- ❀ Do I need to partake in the suggested journal activity to understand what might be blocking my ability to follow through with my agreements/plans?
- ❀ What currently blocks my ability to be in integrity with my word?
- ❀ How will I utilize time to work for me instead of against me?

Chapter 19

Watch Out for the Saboteur

What is this Saboteur, you ask?! In the personal growth field, some refer to it as your "shadow side," others call it your "inner critic," and if that weren't enough nicknames for it, we also have the "sabotager" and the "ego." Whatever you call it, I often say that you know when it's present if you have a certain feeling to give up on all the changes you have been working for and just say , "fuck it all" You just are not in the mood for the lifestyle change you are embarking upon. The dishes are not done, you are behind on work, and everyone around you is asking for your time. Or maybe you find yourself alone often and just don't think that anyone gives a fuck about you or your life.

Now is when you've got to be extra careful! The Saboteur is just waiting in the wings to take you off your new venture and push you back into your old habits. It finds crafty and creative ways to throw you off. So, it can be helpful to picture what your inner saboteur looks like. I like to give it a pirate's hat and a sword as if it feels like it's trying to fight me and cut me down. It's a great opportunity for me to pull out my imaginary sword and fight it back. The way I use my sword against it is with a few key phrases that I have cooked up along the way.

The first one is a phrase that I had you repeat at the beginning of this pocket guide:

"I love you just the way you are now."

It's cheesy, yes, but it's also very effective. You see, each saboteur is a bit different, but what they all have in common is that they like to make you feel like you are not loved and not worth it. The saboteur likes to tempt you with putting things off until tomorrow instead of addressing them today. It likes to coerce you into believing you can't do it and you should just give up. So, you gotta come up with several affirmations and phrases that will combat this little sucker. You see, the saboteur is like a little child who is afraid of change and will fight for things to stay status quo. You can also add in a little phrase for it like, "Change is good as it brings new opportunities that I might really enjoy." Get the saboteur on board with that fact that the unknown; that wonderful mystery of life, is good to experience and that changes are good for you as well. Change really is the only constant in life, so the sooner you can get with that mojo, the smoother your path will be.

Ask Yourself:

- How do I know when my "saboteur" is in effect? What is the energy like of this "inner critic"? What phrases does it use to take me off track?

- What strengths can I draw on to help me overcome this saboteur?

- What phrases/affirmations will serve me in fighting the saboteur?

Chapter 20

Acknowledge and Celebrate Your Progress

O kay, so we all grew up in different times. Maybe as a child, you went to school and they gave out awards at the end of the year for perfect attendance, honor roll and so on. Did you have these awards? Did you earn one or more? Or did you scoff at the kids who earned them? Maybe you didn't have this sort of thing, but you most likely did earn some type of grades while growing up. I remember when I was very young, we received an "S 'for satisfactory, "S+" for a bit better than that, "O" for outstanding and so on. Take a few moments and think back to what the grading system was for you throughout your childhood. What types of grades did you earn and did you care? Did you fit into the system or did you balk at it?

I know I am asking you a lot of questions here but it's important to see how you function when it comes to systems, evaluation measures and progress. You see, many of us do not celebrate or acknowledge ourselves when we are making progress. More often than not, we are looking for the next problem to solve or waiting for the other shoe to drop. It's important to give yourself a "gold star" when you make progress with changing your habits, no matter how small or incremental.

Let's look at some examples. For awhile, I was a teacher and coach for folks who were embarking upon significant health and weight-loss goals. One of the things I noticed over and over again was this overall restriction/all or nothing attitude about it. I would see patients losing weight and feeling better but they would continue to wear the same clothes that they had been wearing for months. Please know I am no fashionista and I do not own that many clothes myself, but if my clothes don't fit, then I've got to get my ass to the store, right?! If you've lost a significant amount of weight and your clothes don't fit but you have a ways to go toward your goal weight, should you purchase some new clothes now or wait until you reach your end goal? The answer: Fuck yes, you need to buy some new clothes now! Why? Because you need new clothes to fit the new you. Why are you waiting until you reach the very end of the goal to give yourself what you need?

I know what you're thinking, "Well Liz, I am not made of money and the clothes I buy now will be too big for me again later so why waste the money?"

No, you are not wasting money; you are rewarding yourself for your progress and you are meeting your needs in the here and now. The overall goal, to me anyways, is to meet your needs in the here and now. That is how you will be able to accept what will be. If you can accept and make decisions off the here and now then you are training yourself at a deeper level to always meet yourself just as you are while you simultaneously move with the only constant in life, which is change.

The other response I would get from clients would be the fear that if they bought the clothes now then they would just give up on their long-term goal and settle at the weight they were at now because they felt good in the clothes they just bought. Well, of course, anything is possible, but what I found was that buying the new clothes midway or so allowed the person to feel a huge boost of self-esteem, confidence and motivation. They were able to truly acknowledge and see their progress and wear their new clothes with confidence. Others would notice, too, and compliments would follow. Please correct me if I am wrong, but I would say that a boosted sense of confidence and self-esteem correlate well with being more successful with progressing towards ones goals! I would also say that rewarding yourself and giving yourself what you need in the present moment is one of the best gifts you can give yourself. It eliminates the old pattern of being restrictive or stingy with your own needs. Practice meeting yourself where you are along the way.

"Don't wait for the end goal to be met before you allow yourself to enjoy your progress".

Make shorter goals and reward yourself along the way for meeting them. Break it down into small portions and attach a gift for yourself when you meet it. I like to break things up into three, five and/or seven-day goals. For example, for this book writing, I gave myself an assignment of writing for 20 minutes per day for 7 days and when I met it, I rewarded myself with a roll up Thai mat. Then I made up my next goal for the next week and so on. The rewards got smaller, but in the beginning I made the reward really big, as I knew it would be toughest to create the consistency of the habit in the beginning.

Ask Yourself:

- How do I reward myself **NOW** for accomplishing the goals that I have met?
- How can I break up my larger goal into smaller, more readily achievable goals?
- What will the rewards be for meeting my smaller goals and how will I keep track of them?
- How can I enjoy the process and progress more on this change path?

Chapter 21

Cues and Triggers

In the psychology world, "triggers" were always these yucky things that none of us wanted to experience. You will know this type of trigger by the talk that often follows about how your mom or dad did this or that to you that was "triggering." It usually relates to some bad experience or memory that has jaded you or left an emotional scar and you might find yourself engaging in the "blame game." Thankfully, in this instance, we are talking about a positive trigger, or what we're going to re-label as a "cue."

Let's look at this in regard to incorporating a new habit into your life. I am sure there have been many times in your past when you have had to take a new medicine or herbal supplement, whether it be temporary or permanent. How did you remember to take it? The cue is the piece that will help you the most with this. For example, you can put a reminder on your phone that will pop up and tell you to take your new herbal supplement. That is considered the "cue," something that is "cueing" you to take it, just like a director says, "action" before the first take. Basically, you have to figure out who and/or what will be your director(s) that will tell you to take "action."

The most effective cues are based in the senses; mainly, they are visual or auditory. For example, when I am taking a new supplement, I leave it out on the cutting board so I will see it each morning when I go to make my breakfast. After a month or so of consistency with remembering to take it, I can put it in the cupboard instead of leaving it out as I am already in the habit of taking it and I may no longer need the cue. However, you may want to keep it on the counter for a long time for ease and to keep up that consistent cueing. You know yourself best, so you get to decide! A familiar auditory cue that I am sure most of you already use is the alarm clock. The sound of the alarm is the cue you set to tell you to wake your ass up and get that day!

Now we've got to address the other side of the cue for when you are focusing on breaking a habit. If you happen to be trying to break the habit of something, this next piece of advisement will appear like a big, "well, duh, Liz" moment, but I've gotta mention it anyway, smarty pants. Have you ever heard the expression, "out of sight, out of mind"? I am sure you have and that is what you will need to do when breaking a habit. You've got to eliminate the cue by getting it out of your sight, out of your auditory space, and so on. If you want to stop eating chips, don't bring them into your home. If someone else in your home MUST have them, then put them in a cupboard that you don't use. Do this for the first month or so, and maybe longer depending on how difficult the habit is for you to break.

Maybe you're trying to break some of your habitual usage of social media. In that case, you can take away a cue by taking it off your phone or other device. I did this with one major social media site that I noticed I was getting all cracky with. I was checking it so many times a day and scrolling and I barely noticed how bad it was until I noticed my energy and mood going in the shitter. So, I deleted it off my phone and told myself that I would not go on it for at least a month. It was so strange to watch how this transition went in the beginning. I would still swipe on my phone to check it but it wasn't there! It was so trippy to truly witness how strong habits are and how it can physically make you search for something out of habit even though you know it's not there! I have to say now what a relief it is to be without that type of social media on my phone. I was able to stick to the one-month mark and it was tough at times because people would ask me if I saw this on there or if they could show me something on it and I would have to tell them that I made an agreement with myself to not connect with it for a month. I am happy to say, It's still off my phone and it's refreshing. I do check in on it on my computer once in awhile but it's in balance and with purpose and it feels good, not cracky!!

Ask yourself:

- Is there a cue you need to create that will support you on your new habit journey?
- Is there a cue you need to eliminate in order to break or lessen a habit you want to get rid of?

Chapter 22

Cravings

lso referred to as a hankering, an urge, an itch, a strong desire, and so on. Sometimes you just gotta have that something when that feeling comes on so strongly, ya know?! Do you ever get those intense cravings for chocolate, maybe a whole pizza, a coffee or a cigarette, maybe even a nice bath?! I could go on for quite awhile about cravings, couldn't you? Here is the deal with cravings: they are not so bad, and in fact they are quite useful. Let's look at an example, shall we?

As I write this, it is a gorgeous Tuesday morning in the winter of 2020, and the world had been battling the COVID-19 pandemic for many months. After I did my yoga and had my breakfast, I decided, for some silly reason, to peruse the news and I discovered that the governor of our state would be doing a live talk on the

Internet. I walked to the kitchen to wash my plate and I had a craving for a drink, yes, of alcohol. Now, it's rare that I have alcohol and I do not drink alcohol in the morning. Yet the thought of what he might deliver for news made me have a craving for a drink! This is even before I watched the damn news report. So, you may be wondering, how could this craving be useful, Liz?

Like this: I was able to notice the craving, link it to the stress/overwhelm of the news delivery, and I was able to choose not to feed the craving. Instead, I acknowledged the feeling behind the craving and chose to take my dog for a walk and reduce any anxiety that was arising. I then decided to watch the governor's talk, but at a different time.

You see, cravings are all too often indicators of what is happening underneath the surface. And sometimes you may be PMS'ing, which is an indicator of your hormones taking over the driver's seat! Other times it's about a memory link. When the governor started to do these talks back in March, my partner and I had a little drink to ease the overwhelm. So in the present moment, I could notice that the craving arose from an association (a memory/happening that occurred awhile back with his talks). You know how that is, you see your drinking buddy walking towards you and all of a sudden you are craving a beer when you were not even thinking of drinking before. Or you get a whiff of some yummy baked good in the air and suddenly you must go home and bake some cookies. Cravings are usually linked to our senses: taste, touch, smell, hearing, and sight. Understanding your senses and how to serve them well with balance is key to working well with this craving game.

A craving can also be an indicator from your body that you are deficient in a vitamin or mineral. Have you ever had an intense craving for something salty? Well, you could be low on sodium. Sometimes the craving is actually your body signaling to you that you are deficient in a vitamin or mineral and you need to take action. Other times, it's simply that old habit that is wanting that sweet or salty taste simply because it is used to having it at certain time of day or because you are used to using it to cope with something or maybe just because! It can be challenging, at times, to decipher whether a craving is truly the sign of a deficiency or something else, yet the more you can understand your inner workings, the easier it gets to understand and work with your cravings.

Remember, cravings are just thoughts and you can ensure they stay that way each time by being aware and unafraid of them! The next time a craving arises, take a moment to check in with your senses and your state of being.

Ask Yourself:

- ❀ Am I feeling balanced in this moment?
- ❀ Do I need some self-soothing? Do I need support? How is my emotional state of being?
- ❀ Do I need the nutrients in the substance I am craving?
- ❀ Ladies, is it that time of the month?

Then Ask Yourself?

- ❀ What is the action I would like to take?
- ❀ Is it best to feed this craving or wait it out and see if it returns?
- ❀ Do I need to see a doctor about my hormonal levels and/or sodium/sugar levels, etc.?

Yes, I listed a lot of questions but you don't have to ask them all at once and over time you won't have to ask these questions because you will understand your inner workings and associations at such a deep level that the choosing and the action and/or inaction becomes so much easier.

Conclusion

Taking Action

Hopefully, you've learned a lot with this pocket guide to habit change. Now, what will you do with these learnings? Or shall I ask, what have you already done with these learnings?! Change takes time and it's a process. Please do honor your process and practice forgiveness towards yourself and others along the way. Do break things down into small steps. Do go easy on yourself. Do celebrate your successes and remember to keep your cheerleaders close by! Don't mind the nay-sayers, they are just jelly. Above all else, be sure to reach out for support when you need it. Community, accountability and connections are essential for creating lasting successful changes. I am here for you with these writings and I am here for you if you decide you could benefit from 1:1 coaching support and classes with me.

You can find me at rootedlivingwellness.com

Enjoy the changes you make and then let it go and take off your evaluator lenses and let yourself live! You got this! You can do this! You are doing this! You ARE worth it!

The END

Bibliography

Maurer, Robert (2014). *The Kaizen Way: One Small Step Can Change Your Life.*

61235971R00061